Daily Rebellion

STUDY GUIDE

Cover design by: Sara Young
Cover photo by: Andrew van Tilborgh

ISBN: 978-1-964794-53-2   1 2 3 4 5 6 7 8 9 10

Printed in the United States of America

Daily
Rebellion

STUDY GUIDE

Kevin S. Taylor

AVAIL

Contents

Daily
Rebellion

The Everyday
Fight to Press Pause

Includes 60-minute practices to quiet
the noise and strengthen your soul.

Kevin S. Taylor

Introduction

Rebellion doesn't have to be loud or flashy. It can actually be quiet and gentle.

Review, Reflect, and Respond

As you read the Introduction in Daily Rebellion, *review, reflect on, and respond to the text by answering the following questions.*

What would it mean for you to see soul care not as indulgence, but as sacred resistance—and are you ready to live that way?

_____

_____

_____

_____

_____

_____

_____

_____

_____

_____

What weight are you holding right now that you know you can't carry much longer?

_____

_____

_____

_____

_____

_____

_____

_____

_____

How willing are you to be honest with yourself in this journey—especially when the pause reveals things you'd rather avoid?

_____

_____

_____

_____

_____

_____

_____

_____

_____

_____

What kind of transformation do you hope to experience as you engage with this book—and how committed are you to doing the soul work it invites you into?

_____

_____

_____

_____

_____

_____

_____

_____

_____

_____

The Everyday
Fight to Press Pause

Here the Rebellion Began

There's a hole, if not on the soul-care shelf at the library, in our hearts.

Review, Reflect, and Respond

READING TIME *As you read Chapter 1: "Here the Rebellion Began" in Daily Rebellion, review, reflect on, and respond to the text by answering the following questions.*

What stood out to you most about the author's first silent prayer retreat—and how did his experience challenge or encourage your perspective on stillness?

_____

_____

_____

_____

_____

_____

_____

_____

_____

How do you currently define "pressing pause," and how often do you make space for it in your daily routine?

_____

_____

_____

_____

_____

_____

_____

_____

_____

> **"Come to me, all you who are weary and burdened, and I will give you rest."**
>
> **—Matthew 11:28 (NIV)**

Consider the scripture above and answer the following questions:

When you read the word "rest" in this verse, what kind of rest does your soul most crave right now—emotional, spiritual, physical, mental? What would it sound like to ask Jesus for that specific kind of rest today?

_____

_____

_____

_____

_____

_____

_____

_____

How does this verse affirm the idea that soul care is not selfish but sacred? How does it challenge the way you structure your time and priorities each day?

_____

_____

_____

_____

_____

_____

_____

_____

Everyone has moments of weariness—but not everyone is willing to admit it. What indicators in your own life signal when your soul is running on empty?

_____

_____

_____

_____

_____

_____

_____

Have you ever found yourself ministering or leading from a place of dryness, depletion, or being overwhelmed? What did you learn from that season?

_____

_____

_____

_____

_____

_____

In what ways have you experienced guilt or internal resistance to pausing—even when you knew your soul needed it?

_____

_____

_____

_____

_____

_____

How do these everyday pauses—like muting on Zoom or taking the long way home—challenge the belief that you don't have time to pause? What does that reveal about what's truly possible when it comes to creating intentional space for your soul?

_____

_____

_____

_____

_____

_____

What do your current daily habits say about the priority (or lack thereof) you place on your soul?

_____

_____

_____

_____

_____

_____

What reasons do you tend to give yourself for pushing through—even when you sense your soul is asking you to slow down?

_____

_____

_____

_____

_____

_____

_____

_____

If someone close to you were to audit your pace, your pauses, and your presence over the last seven days, what would they conclude about the condition of your soul?

_____

_____

_____

_____

_____

_____

_____

What does your reaction to the pause hack—sitting in silence with your morning drink—reveal about your comfort with stillness?

_____

_____

_____

_____

_____

_____

_____

Rebel With a Pause

*Every time I choose the pause
over the output, I become
a rebel (of the best sort).*

Review, Reflect, and Respond

READING TIME *As you read Chapter 2: "Rebel With a Pause" in* Daily Rebellion, *review, reflect on, and respond to the text by answering the following questions.*

Where do you feel most worn down in ways that sleep or rest can't fix—and what does that reveal about your soul?

_____

_____

_____

_____

_____

_____

_____

_____

This chapter compares pausing to an act of protest. How might that perspective reshape the way you think about stillness?

_____

_____

_____

_____

_____

_____

_____

_____

> *"Then they sat on the ground with him for seven days and seven nights. No one said a word to him, because they saw how great his suffering was."*
>
> **—Job 2:13 (NIV)**

Consider the scripture above and answer the following questions:

When have you struggled to sit in silence with someone who was hurting—and what made it uncomfortable or difficult?

_____

_____

_____

_____

_____

_____

_____

_____

How does this verse challenge your tendency to fill silence with words, productivity, or distraction?

_____

_____

_____

_____

_____

_____

_____

_____

_____

What fear, belief, or pressure might be behind the excuses you make for avoiding meaningful pauses?

_____

_____

_____

_____

_____

_____

_____

The chapter describes a moment of quiet writing during Jesus's encounter with the adulterous woman. What does that kind of thoughtful pause teach you about the role of restraint and reflection in tense situations?

_____

_____

_____

_____

_____

_____

Think back to a moment when you acted or spoke too quickly—how might a pause have changed the outcome?

_____

_____

_____

_____

_____

_____

Which type of pause do you most resist: physical (rest), emotional (feeling), mental (slowing your thoughts), or spiritual (prayer)? Why do you think that's the case?

_____

_____

_____

_____

_____

_____

_____

_____

_____

The "Selah" metaphor invites us to let the ripples of life settle before moving on. When was the last time you waited long enough for the water to go still—and what happened when you did?

_____

_____

_____

_____

_____

_____

_____

_____

_____

The story of Abel and the rabbi in this chapter offers a picture of how pausing deepens understanding. What practical steps can you take to slow down and "hear the music of heaven" this week?

_____

_____

_____

_____

_____

_____

_____

_____

What part of the 1-hour soul pause impacted you most—and what part was most difficult to engage with? Why?

_____

_____

_____

_____

_____

_____

_____

_____

_____

_____

Still Waters, Wild Grace

The Good Shepherd doesn't just want you unstuck; He wants you to be revitalized so your soul can prosper.

Review, Reflect, and Respond

As you read Chapter 3: "Still Waters, Wild Grace" in Daily Rebellion, *review, reflect on, and respond to the text by answering the following questions.*

What images or moments from the shepherd parables in this chapter stayed with you—and why?

_____

_____

_____

_____

_____

_____

_____

The chapter compares our spiritual condition to sheep—easily distracted, often afraid, and stubbornly resistant to rest. Where have you seen these traits in your own life lately?

_____

_____

_____

_____

_____

_____

_____

_____

_____

_____

> *"The LORD is my shepherd, I lack nothing. He makes me lie down in green pastures, he leads me beside quiet waters, he refreshes my soul."*
>
> **—Psalm 23:1-4 (NIV)**

Consider the scripture above and answer the following questions:

The Shepherd "makes us lie down"—even when we resist. When has God prompted you to pause, and how did you respond?

_____

_____

_____

_____

_____

_____

_____

_____

When has the Shepherd led you beside "quiet waters"? What did that moment of restoration feel like?

_____

_____

_____

_____

_____

_____

_____

_____

The story of the shepherd counting his sheep by name reminds us that we are known and pursued. When have you felt like the "one" that wandered—and how did God meet you?

_____

_____

_____

_____

_____

_____

_____

The author highlights four things sheep need in order to lie down: freedom from fear, friction, pests, and hunger. Which of these most often keeps your soul from resting?

_____

_____

_____

_____

_____

_____

_____

What "flies" (daily irritations, distractions, mental noise) do you need the Shepherd to anoint and quiet in this season?

_____

_____

_____

_____

_____

_____

How has God used a season of "wilderness" in your life to redirect you toward something better—even if it didn't feel good at the time?

_____

_____

_____

_____

_____

_____

_____

_____

Which part of the Shepherd's care—leading, refreshing, or guiding—do you most need to trust right now? Craft a personal prayer asking the Shepherd to meet you in that specific area, help you surrender control, and remind you that His presence is enough.

_____

_____

_____

_____

_____

_____

_____

_____

The chapter closes with an invitation to embrace wild grace and soul care rooted in the Shepherd's character. What hinders you from receiving that grace fully?

_____

_____

_____

_____

_____

_____

_____

_____

_____

_____

What part of the 1-hour soul pause impacted you most—and what part was most difficult to engage with?

_____

_____

_____

_____

_____

_____

_____

_____

_____

Who's Your Doppelganger?

Not only did God knit and create your soul; He knitted it in His image.

Review, Reflect, and Respond

READING TIME *As you read Chapter 4: "Who's Your Doppelganger?" in* Daily Rebellion, *review, reflect on, and respond to the text by answering the following questions.*

What part of Chapter 4 challenged or inspired you most—and why?

_____

_____

_____

_____

_____

_____

_____

_____

When was the last time you truly paused to reflect on your God-given identity? What did that moment reveal to you about how you see yourself—and how God sees you?

_____

_____

_____

_____

_____

_____

_____

_____

> **"Then God said, 'Let us make mankind in our image, in our likeness, so that they may rule over the fish in the sea and the birds in the sky, over the livestock and all the wild animals and over all the creatures that move along the ground.'"**
>
> **—Genesis 1:26 (NIV)**

Consider the scripture above and answer the following questions:

What does it mean to you that you were made in the image and likeness of God?

_____

_____

_____

_____

_____

_____

_____

Where do you struggle most to believe that your value is already secured by your Creator—and how might living from your imago Dei identity change the way you engage with those parts of your life this week?

_____

_____

_____

_____

_____

_____

_____

Have you ever felt like just a "role" or a "title" instead of a soul? How did that realization affect you? How is it affecting you now?

_____

_____

_____

_____

_____

_____

When the team member said, "I have a soul too," what did that moment stir in you? Can you recall a time when you or someone around you felt unseen in this way?

_____

_____

_____

_____

_____

_____

Are there people in your life or organization who may not hold leadership titles but carry heavy spiritual or emotional loads? How might you offer them space for soul care?

_____

_____

_____

_____

_____

_____

Have you ever tried to "duplicate" yourself—perhaps by overextending, multitasking, or leading on autopilot? What would it look like to let go of that version and simply be God's original design?

_____

_____

_____

_____

_____

_____

_____

_____

The chapter describes how certain "quirks" reflected generational imprints. What are some aspects of your personality or habits that feel deeply rooted—and how might they reflect God's creative intention?

_____

_____

_____

_____

_____

_____

_____

_____

_____

If you really believed your life's purpose is to glorify the One who made you, what practical change would you make to how you live or lead this week?

_____

_____

_____

_____

_____

_____

_____

_____

_____

What part of the 1-hour soul pause impacted you most—and what part was most difficult to engage with?

_____

_____

_____

_____

_____

_____

_____

_____

_____

_____

Lessons in Horticulture

God's melody over us is not a dirge of disappointment or frustration—it's a song of love.

Review, Reflect, and Respond

As you read Chapter 5: "Lessons in Horticulture" in Daily Rebellion, *review, reflect on, and respond to the text by answering the following questions.*

What part of the chapter's vineyard imagery—like the pruning process or remaining connected to the vine—caught your attention the most and why?

_____

_____

_____

_____

_____

_____

_____

_____

Have you ever experienced a season of "spiritual pruning"? How did it feel at the time, and what fruit—if any—emerged afterward?

_____

_____

_____

_____

_____

_____

_____

_____

_____

_____

> **"He cuts off every branch in me that bears no fruit, while every branch that does bear fruit he prunes so it will be even more fruitful."**
>
> **—John 15:2 (NIV)**

Consider the scripture above and answer the following questions:

How does this verse apply to your life, and how does it challenge your view of hardship or difficulty?

_____

_____

_____

_____

_____

_____

_____

_____

What might God be trying to prune in your life right now—and how are you responding to that pruning?

_____

_____

_____

_____

_____

_____

_____

_____

_____

What are some "fruitless branches" in your life right now—habits, patterns, relationships, or pursuits—that may need to be surrendered in order for more fruit to grow?

_____

_____

_____

_____

_____

_____

_____

Where do you feel overwhelmed in your walk with Jesus, and how might the practice of pausing relieve that burden?

_____

_____

_____

_____

_____

_____

What part of "remaining in the Vine" do you find most difficult: creating space, slowing down, trusting God's timing, or letting go of control? Why?

_____

_____

_____

_____

_____

_____

_____

_____

What false narratives about performance-based spirituality do you need to uproot in order to remain in Christ more fully?

_____

_____

_____

_____

_____

_____

_____

_____

_____

What fruits of the Spirit (Galatians 5:22-23) have been growing in your life lately? Which feel underdeveloped—and how might pruning help them flourish?

_____

_____

_____

_____

_____

_____

_____

_____

_____

_____

_____

What signs in your life let you know when you're living disconnected from the Vine?

_____

_____

_____

_____

_____

_____

_____

_____

_____

What part of the 1-hour soul pause impacted you most—and what part was most difficult to engage with?

_____

_____

_____

_____

_____

_____

_____

_____

_____

_____

Wave a White Flag

Waving the white flag to Jesus means letting grace do what grit never could.

Review, Reflect, and Respond

READING TIME *As you read Chapter 6: "Wave a White Flag" in Daily Rebellion, review, reflect on, and respond to the text by answering the following questions.*

What emotion rises in you when you hear the word surrender—and where do you think that emotion comes from?

_____

_____

_____

_____

_____

_____

_____

_____

What area of your life have you held onto for too long, hoping your strength or strategy would be enough?

_____

_____

_____

_____

_____

_____

_____

_____

_____

"If anyone would come after me, let him deny himself and take up his cross daily and follow me. For whoever would save his life will lose it, but whoever loses his life for my sake will save it."

—Luke 9:23-24 (ESV)

Consider the scripture above and answer the following questions:

"Daily" surrender is often harder than dramatic, one-time acts of sacrifice. What would daily surrender look like in a specific area of your life this week?

_____

_____

_____

_____

_____

_____

Jesus says, "Whoever loses his life for my sake will save it." What part of your identity, comfort, or control are you afraid to lose—even if it means discovering something deeper with Him?

_____

_____

_____

_____

_____

_____

In your own words, how does the practice of pausing connect with surrender?

_____

_____

_____

_____

_____

_____

When was the last time you paused long enough to ask God what He wants to shape in you—and what needs to be laid down?

_____

_____

_____

_____

_____

_____

Where is God asking you to obey before you understand?

_____

_____

_____

_____

_____

_____

_____

Surrender is described as a rebellion against the values of the world. In what ways does your life reflect that kind of holy rebellion—and where does it still blend in?

_____

_____

_____

_____

_____

_____

_____

_____

What is one memory of God's provision or presence you need to bring back to the forefront today?

_____

_____

_____

_____

_____

_____

_____

_____

_____

Jesus doesn't invite us into comfort, but into cross-carrying. What "cross" are you currently being invited to carry, and how are you responding?

_____

_____

_____

_____

_____

_____

_____

_____

_____

What part of the 1-hour soul pause impacted you most—and what part was most difficult to engage with?

_____

_____

_____

_____

_____

_____

_____

_____

_____

_____

Wait for It

Getting filled up isn't the issue as much as what you fill yourself with.

Review, Reflect, and Respond

As you read Chapter 7: "Wait for It" in Daily Rebellion, *review, reflect on, and respond to the text by answering the following questions.*

The chapter draws a contrast between being filled with the Holy Spirit and simply being a believer. In what areas of your life do you need more than belief—you need to be filled?

_____

_____

_____

_____

_____

_____

_____

_____

_____

When was a time something went wrong in your life but ended up drawing you closer to God?

_____

_____

_____

_____

_____

_____

_____

_____

_____

_____

> *"Whether you turn to the right or to the left, your ears will hear a voice behind you, saying, 'This is the way; walk in it.'"*
>
> **—Isaiah 30:21 (NIV)**

Consider the scripture above and answer the following questions:

This scripture speaks of a voice guiding us in real-time. When was a moment you sensed the Holy Spirit nudging you in one direction—or holding you back from another?

_____

_____

_____

_____

_____

_____

This verse suggests that divine guidance can come even after you've started moving. Where in your life are you holding back, waiting for clear answers from God, instead of taking a step of faith?

_____

_____

_____

_____

_____

_____

_____

What are you currently filling your heart and mind with—and how is it impacting your spiritual life?

_____

_____

_____

_____

_____

_____

_____

The chapter identifies the Spirit as Convictor, Guide, and Comforter. Which of these roles do you most need right now—and which are you resisting?

_____

_____

_____

_____

_____

_____

_____

Have you ever treated the Holy Spirit more like a "force" than a person? How does that perception shape the way you pray or listen?

_____

_____

_____

_____

_____

_____

The chapter asks, "Have you been filled with the Spirit?"—not "Are you behaving correctly?" How does this shift your view of spiritual maturity?

_____

_____

_____

_____

_____

_____

_____

_____

How have you seen the Holy Spirit transform someone's life—and what did that change look like?

_____

_____

_____

_____

_____

_____

_____

_____

_____

What does a meaningful "pause" with the Holy Spirit look like for you right now—and how will you make space for it?

_____

_____

_____

_____

_____

_____

_____

_____

_____

What part of the 1-hour soul pause impacted you most—and what part was most difficult to engage with?

_____

_____

_____

_____

_____

_____

_____

_____

_____

_____

To Listen or Not to Listen . . . That Is the Question

*Sometimes the hard way
is the right way.*

Review, Reflect, and Respond

As you read Chapter 8: "To Listen or Not to Listen . . . That Is the Question" in Daily Rebellion, *review, reflect on, and respond to the text by answering the following questions.*

How would you honestly rate your ability to recognize and respond to God's voice—and how might your current pace of life be affecting your ability to hear Him clearly?

_____

_____

_____

_____

_____

_____

_____

We rarely hear people say, "I want to be a better listener." When was the last time you expressed that desire, and how might this reveal an area of spiritual immaturity or maturity in your walk with God?

_____

_____

_____

_____

_____

_____

_____

_____

> *"However, if you do not obey the LORD your God and do not carefully follow all his commands and decrees I am giving you today, all these curses will come on you and overtake you."*
>
> **—Deuteronomy 28:15 (NIV)**

Consider the scripture above and answer the following questions:

How does this verse confront your current attitude toward obedience? In what area of life do you know what God is asking—but continue to delay or ignore it?

_____

_____

_____

_____

_____

_____

What does it mean to "carefully follow" in your daily rhythms—and how does this contrast with selective or convenient listening?

_____

_____

_____

_____

_____

_____

_____

When have you mistaken your own desire or emotion for the voice of God? How did you eventually discern the difference?

_____

_____

_____

_____

_____

_____

When was the last time you paused and truly asked God to speak to you—and waited for an answer? What happened?

_____

_____

_____

_____

_____

_____

What regular practices do you have in place to create space for hearing God's voice—such as silence, journaling, or intentional reflection?

_____

_____

_____

_____

_____

_____

In the story of Samuel, it took Eli's help for him to recognize God's voice. Who in your life helps you discern what God might be saying—and how open are you to their counsel?

_____

_____

_____

_____

_____

_____

_____

_____

_____

In what specific ways has past obedience strengthened your faith or changed your trajectory?

_____

_____

_____

_____

_____

_____

_____

_____

_____

What specific distractions most often drown out God's voice in your day—and what will you commit to turning off or tuning out this week?

_____

_____

_____

_____

_____

_____

_____

_____

_____

What part of the S.O.A.P. method in the 1-hour soul pause application (Scripture, Observation, Application, Prayer) do you find most difficult—and why might that be?

_____

_____

_____

_____

_____

_____

_____

_____

_____

Keeping Sabbath

We are different people going into Sabbath than we are coming out of Sabbath.

Review, Reflect, and Respond

READING TIME *As you read Chapter 9: "Keeping Sabbath" in* Daily Rebellion, *review, reflect on, and respond to the text by answering the following questions.*

What words, phrases, concepts, or practices from this chapter on Sabbath stuck with you most—and why?

_____

_____

_____

_____

_____

_____

_____

_____

When you think about "keeping Sabbath," does your first reaction feel inviting or intimidating? Explain why.

_____

_____

_____

_____

_____

_____

_____

_____

_____

> **"There remains, then, a Sabbath-rest for the people of God; for anyone who enters God's rest also rests from their works, just as God did from his."**
>
> **—Hebrews 4:9-10 (NIV)**

Consider the scripture above and answer the following questions:

According to this passage, God's rest is still available—what does that say about how seriously He takes rest, even today, and why?

_____

_____

_____

_____

_____

_____

How does this passage challenge your current understanding of success, productivity, or spiritual maturity—and what fears might be shaping those definitions?

_____

_____

_____

_____

_____

_____

_____

The chapter says, "Sabbath isn't about increased pressure or greater performance. It's about permission." What's one area in your life where you've been treating rest as a reward instead of a right?

_____

_____

_____

_____

_____

_____

_____

Which part of the Jewish Sabbath practice challenged or inspired you most—and how could you begin adapting a similar rhythm in your own life?

_____

_____

_____

_____

_____

_____

What false narratives are you still believing about what gives you value?

_____

_____

_____

_____

_____

_____

_____

What practical steps could you take this week to prepare for a Sabbath pause, even if it's just for a few hours? What needs to change in your schedule or mindset?

_____

_____

_____

_____

_____

_____

_____

_____

_____

When was the last time you experienced true rest—not just physical stillness, but deep soul-level restoration? What made it possible—and why haven't you returned to that space?

_____

_____

_____

_____

_____

_____

_____

_____

_____

_____

What are you most afraid might happen if you really stopped and rested?

_____

_____

_____

_____

_____

_____

_____

_____

_____

Which of the Sabbath practices or time-specific rhythms in the soul pause application feels most realistic for you to commit to right now? What would need to shift in your week to make it happen?

_____

_____

_____

_____

_____

_____

_____

_____

_____

_____

"Carousel" Got It Right

Walking alone makes the burdens heavier and the victories emptier.

Review, Reflect, and Respond

READING TIME **As you read Chapter 10: "'Carousel' Got It Right" in** Daily Rebellion, *review, reflect on, and respond to the text by answering the following questions.*

What did your responses to the 10-point assessment reveal about the current state of your community life? Were you surprised, pleased, or unsettled by any of your ratings—and what specific areas did it highlight as strengths or areas for growth?

_____

_____

_____

_____

_____

_____

_____

What specific aspect of true community—shared burdens, encouragement, or accountability—do you feel you need most right now?

_____

_____

_____

_____

_____

_____

_____

_____

_____

> *"Two are better than one, because they have a good return for their labor. If either of them falls down, one can help the other up. But pity anyone who falls and has no one to help them up."*
>
> **—Ecclesiastes 4:9-10 (NIV)**

Consider the scripture above and answer the following questions:

Ecclesiastes speaks to the value of having someone to help us when we fall. When was the last time you leaned on someone, and how did their presence or support change your situation?

_____

_____

_____

_____

_____

_____

_____

How does this scripture challenge you to invest more intentionally in community, both in times of need and in celebration?

_____

_____

_____

_____

_____

_____

_____

When have you gone out of your way to help someone, even when it wasn't convenient?

_____

_____

_____

_____

_____

_____

_____

How does your pace of life and relationships affect your ability to pause and be present with others?

_____

_____

_____

_____

_____

_____

_____

The chapter highlights how community helps us heal, grow, and thrive. What barriers or fears prevent you from fully participating in your community of faith, and how can you address them?

_____

_____

_____

_____

_____

_____

_____

How do you handle moments of tension in your community? Provide an example. How might pausing to reflect and engage in humility change the outcomes of those situations?

_____

_____

_____

_____

_____

_____

_____

_____

_____

_____

What does your community look like right now, and what role are you actively playing in it?

_____

_____

_____

_____

_____

_____

_____

_____

_____

How does your community reflect both the strengths and the challenges of its members? In what ways might the differences and challenges within your community actually be part of its strength?

_____

_____

_____

_____

_____

_____

_____

_____

_____

What part of the 1-hour soul pause impacted you most—and what part was most difficult to engage with?

_____

_____

_____

_____

_____

_____

_____

_____

_____

CHAPTER 11

Happy Trails
to You

*Sometimes the most unexpected
beauty comes not from what is
present, but from what is absent.*

Review, Reflect, and Respond

READING TIME *As you read Chapter 11: "Happy Trails to You" in Daily Rebellion, review, reflect on, and respond to the text by answering the following questions.*

When was the last time you intentionally paused to connect with God through nature—and what did that moment stir in you?

_____

_____

_____

_____

_____

_____

_____

_____

_____

What specific part of creation most often draws you into wonder or helps you feel close to God?

_____

_____

_____

_____

_____

_____

_____

_____

_____

_____

> *"How many are your works, LORD! In wisdom you made them all; the earth is full of your creatures. There is the sea, vast and spacious, teeming with creatures beyond number—living things both large and small."*
>
> **—Psalm 104:24-25 (NIV)**

Consider the scripture above and answer the following questions:

How does your experience of nature deepen your awareness of God's presence?

_____

_____

_____

_____

_____

_____

_____

Think about the last time you felt awe in creation. What did that moment teach you about your place in God's design?

_____

_____

_____

_____

_____

_____

_____

The chapter describes creation as "preaching all the time." What messages might God be speaking to you through the natural world that you've been too busy to hear?

_____

_____

_____

_____

_____

_____

_____

We often wait for a "more spiritual" setting before we engage with God. How does that mindset limit your ability to meet with Him in everyday surroundings?

_____

_____

_____

_____

_____

_____

_____

Which metaphor or imagery from nature in this chapter spoke to something specific in your current season of life?

_____

_____

_____

_____

_____

_____

_____

What obstacles—internal or external—keep you from getting outside and being with God in creation more regularly?

_____

_____

_____

_____

_____

_____

_____

_____

We're reminded that Jesus withdrew into nature often. What can you learn from His example about rest, focus, and communion with God?

_____

_____

_____

_____

_____

_____

_____

_____

_____

What's one way you can begin recovering a sense of wonder in your walk with God this week?

_____

_____

_____

_____

_____

_____

_____

_____

_____

_____

What part of the 75-minute soul pause impacted you most—and what part was most difficult to engage with?

_____

_____

_____

_____

_____

_____

_____

_____

_____

_____

CHAPTER 12

The Gift of Now

*Gratitude doesn't need
to be dramatic. It just
needs to be genuine.*

Review, Reflect, and Respond

As you read Chapter 12: "The Gift of Now" in Daily Rebellion, *review, reflect on, and respond to the text by answering the following questions.*

How did the story of Paul and Silas reshape your perspective on worshiping in the middle of hardship—and how easy or difficult is it for you to do that in your own life, and why?

_____

_____

_____

_____

_____

_____

_____

_____

_____

In what areas of your life are you currently being invited to offer gratitude before the breakthrough? What would that look and sound like?

_____

_____

_____

_____

_____

_____

_____

_____

_____

> *"I will sing of the LORD's great love forever; with my mouth I will make your faithfulness known through all generations. I will declare that your love stands firm forever, that you have established your faithfulness in heaven itself."*
>
> **—Psalm 89:1-2 (NIV)**

Consider the scripture above and answer the following questions:

This passage proclaims the Lord's love and faithfulness. How can you declare His faithfulness today, even if your circumstances haven't changed?

_____

_____

_____

_____

_____

_____

What role does singing or vocal expression play in your ability to shift your mindset toward gratitude and hope?

_____

_____

_____

_____

_____

_____

_____

What ordinary things in your life do you now recognize as extraordinary blessings after reading this chapter?

_____

_____

_____

_____

_____

_____

Consider the story of Jonah. How do you relate to the idea of "the belly" being both a confinement and a gift? What did it make you reflect on in your own life?

_____

_____

_____

_____

_____

_____

Which suggestions for cultivating gratitude (journaling, worship, out-loud thanks, serving, etc.) are most accessible for you to start practicing this week?

_____

_____

_____

_____

_____

_____

When you think about the story of the one leper who returned, what does it say about your own tendency to move on versus return with thankfulness?

_____

_____

_____

_____

_____

_____

_____

_____

_____

How did the chapter's retelling of Corrie ten Boom's story challenge your assumptions about what God can be thanked for?

_____

_____

_____

_____

_____

_____

_____

_____

_____

What do you think it means to be "made whole" versus just "healed," and how can gratitude play a role in your own wholeness?

_____

_____

_____

_____

_____

_____

_____

_____

What part of the 1-hour soul pause impacted you most—and what part was most difficult to engage with?

_____

_____

_____

_____

_____

_____

_____

_____

_____

_____

When the Ground Shifts Beneath You

*When something comes
into your life that forces you
to pause, your humanity
comes into sharper focus.*

Review, Reflect, and Respond

READING TIME *As you read Chapter 13: "When the Ground Shifts Beneath You" in* Daily Rebellion, *review, reflect on, and respond to the text by answering the following questions.*

When have you experienced a forced pause in life, and how did it shape or shift your perspective?

_____

_____

_____

_____

_____

_____

_____

_____

The chapter explores a journey from fear to trust. Where are you in that journey right now—and what past wound or personal belief might be making that journey more difficult?

_____

_____

_____

_____

_____

_____

_____

_____

_____

_____

> *"My grace is sufficient for you, for my power is made perfect in weakness. Therefore I will boast all the more gladly about my weaknesses, so that Christ's power may rest on me. That is why, for Christ's sake, I delight in weaknesses, in insults, in hardships, in persecutions, in difficulties. For when I am weak, then I am strong."*
>
> **—2 Corinthians 12:9-10 (NIV)**

Consider the scripture above and answer the following questions:

How does Paul's view of weakness in 2 Corinthians 12:9-10 differ from the way weakness is often viewed in our culture?

_____

_____

_____

_____

_____

_____

_____

"My grace is sufficient for you." In what area of your life do you most doubt that God's grace is enough—and why?

_____

_____

_____

_____

_____

_____

_____

When everything feels out of your control, where do you typically place your trust—and has that proven reliable?

_____

_____

_____

_____

_____

_____

How have you seen pain become a teacher in your life? And where are you still resisting its lessons?

_____

_____

_____

_____

_____

_____

What part of you has become addicted to striving or pushing through—afraid of what might surface if you really paused?

_____

_____

_____

_____

_____

_____

In what ways are you waiting for healing before you believe you can have peace or purpose?

_____

_____

_____

_____

_____

_____

_____

What emotions or fears do you suppress in the name of "being strong," and what would it cost you to stop pretending?

_____

_____

_____

_____

_____

_____

_____

What story are you telling yourself about your current season—and is it a story of fear, frustration, or faith?

_____

_____

_____

_____

_____

_____

_____

_____

What part of the 1-hour soul pause impacted you most—and
what part was most difficult to engage with?

_____

_____

_____

_____

_____

_____

_____

Looking back on your journey through this book, what has
God revealed to you about your need for pause—and how has
that changed the way you see yourself, your pace, and His
presence in your everyday life?

_____

_____

_____

_____

_____

_____

_____

_____

www.ingramcontent.com/pod-product-compliance
Lightning Source LLC
Chambersburg PA
CBHW062119080426
42734CB00012B/2915